SWOT Analysis Supercharged
By
Robert Villegas

SWOT Analysis Supercharged

By Robert Villegas

© Copyright 2017 by Robert Villegas

All rights reserved. No part of this book may be reproduced in any form without the prior written consent of the copyright holder and/or his representative/s.

Published in the United States of America by Document Services International

Series Title: Villegas Business Volume 2

www.robertvillegas.com

Contact: **robertsswot@outlook.com**

ISBN-13: 978-1979590372

ISBN-10: 1979590370

Social Media Addresses

Parler: **@Robertv1989**
CloutHub @RobertVillegas
MeWe Robert Villegas
Minds @Robertv1989
Gab @V4Vendata

Table of Contents

WHAT IS A SWOT ANALYSIS? 4
HISTORY OF THE SWOT ANALYSIS 6
SMART GOALS 8
SWOT Analysis 10
DECISION-MAKING WORKSHEET 42
PROBLEM SOLVING WORKSHEET 47
SWOT ANALYSIS AS A PERFORMANCE REVIEW 53
THE PERSONAL SWOT ANALYSIS 55
CONCLUSION 57

What is a SWOT Analysis?

Your company has a problem. This problem has arisen during the course of doing business as usual. It is something you may not have envisioned when you started the company; but it has come up and must be dealt with if your company is to continue to improve. Many employees have noticed it and they have asked that something be done about it. In fact, it is such a big problem that it threatens the success of the business and customers have started complaining.

Now, you, the business owner, are confronted with a major issue. What do you do about this problem? How are you going to make the problem go away?

A SWOT Analysis is an objective look at the internal and external elements of your organization that impact your success or lack thereof. If done diligently, you will always have a handle on what you need to do to improve season after season. At the very least, this analysis should be done at the end of each year (or after each major event).

By analyzing and understanding the internal resources available in planning your coming year, you will gain a better understanding of what you need to do to take advantage of **S**trengths and how to overcome **W**eaknesses. Understanding and planning for both **O**pportunities and **T**hreats will give you crucial information for assessing external situations that impact your business, local communities and the field in which you work.

History of the SWOT Analysis

The first SWOT Analysis was probably done on a long-ago veranda by an enterprising hunter who had just failed to make the "big kill". More than likely, this hunter took stock of everything that had just transpired during the hunt. He looked at his strengths as a hunter, his weaknesses, what opportunities he had to improve and how to assess the threats brought to the hunt by the reluctant prey.

When he looked at his strengths, he assessed his speed, his physical abilities, and his brain power. He identified the strengths he could improve to be a better hunter next time. He also looked at his weaknesses and determined which of these he could eliminate. He looked at his tools and how to improve them. He could make a sharper blade on his spear or a bigger stick. These presented new opportunities to be a great hunter. Finally, he analyzed his prey to determine how to take advantage of its weakness or how to develop a smarter strategy for capturing it in the future.

He learned he could do this assessment after every hunt and become an even better hunter over time while capturing bigger prey with much less energy. His approach was very logical and what he learned helped him get closer to the "big kill" if he was diligent.

He would be so successful, he and his family would be better fed and he would enjoy telling his friends and family about the hunt while they sat around the fire after dinner. He even imagined his own image reflected on the cave wall while he lifted a large bone over his head and simulated the final blow that did the beast in. Life was good for the successful hunter.

Today, this very same approach has been distilled into what college professors call the SWOT Analysis and it can be applied to virtually any situation in any business entity and even in one's career. The hunter is still turning on his mind and focusing on his own strengths, weaknesses, opportunities and threats as he performs his every-day activities. Now the SWOT Analysis is a staple of the business world, and it has been perfected countless times by business owners and their employees.

SMART Goals

Additionally, if you apply the SMART rules and integrate them into the SWOT Analysis, you can improve your prospects of success even more. SMART stands for Specific, Measurable, Achievable, Results-Focused and Time-bound goals. For instance, if you take a goal that you've developed out of a Weakness and make it Specific, Measurable, Achievable, Results-Focused and Time-bound, you can make some significant changes that will actually work for you.

Regarding this goal:

Specific: Sell more can openers.

Measurable: Sell 10 more can openers

Achievable: Yes, by explaining features better (Weakness: Does not explain features fully)

Results-Focused: Yes

Time-bound: next week and thereafter

As you can see, the integration of SWOT and SMART goals can improve sales which increases production and profits for the company. The manager can then advance to the step of informing his supervisors to ensure that every employee is able to fully explain all product features in order to increase the overall effectiveness of the sales department. The data gathered from the SWOT Analysis in all categories can create a number of SMART goals which can be implemented company-wide creating more sales and increasing job security and employee confidence.

I have written this book to take an "old school" concept like the "SWOT Analysis" and supercharge it with the concept of SMART goals. Through this approach, you will gain new insights, not only into your markets, but possible other markets as well as new directions your company can take. By developing SMART goals, you will be able to innovate in your company to a degree commonly not thought possible. Your results will be measurable and reportable to upper management as successes and improvements.

If you have new ideas or suggestions to add to this concept, by all means, let me know by emailing me at **robertsswot@outlook.com**. I guarantee that if your idea is added to future volumes of the book, you will receive complete credit.

Onward.

SWOT Analysis

THE STRENGTHS, WEAKNESSES, OPPORTUNITIES AND THREATS ANALYSIS

One thing few companies do today is conduct a **S**trengths, **W**eaknesses, **O**pportunities, and **T**hreats (SWOT) analysis on their company or on any specific aspect of their business. Yet, regular and consistent analyses of this type can be critical to future success.

Needless to say, before you conduct your SWOT analysis, you must be familiar with every detail of your business and potential weaknesses in your organization, including budget, personnel, volunteers/interns, time, schedule, series target audiences, and population sizes of the communities where you do business. If you are not, then enlist the time and expertise of the individual you have delegated to perform these activities.

The first thing to do is set up a meeting with your general management staff. You want to ask each of them about their biggest problem area to get a good idea of the direction you want to take your first SWOT Analysis. Ask what one problem they would want fixed that would most impact their ability to serve the customer or improve production or lower prices. Take careful notes about who makes which suggestion and get input from the group about which specific problem would be most effective to solve. Gather your notes and then meet with each individual separately and ask him if he were in charge of a specific project, how would he go about running a project team to work on the problem.

Strengths

What distinct competencies does your organization bring to your field? Is there anything unique about you that gives you an advantage you can exploit that would continue to give you an edge, or as Penske would say, to give you the unfair advantage? What additional competencies are possessed by your key employees that might give you an advantage? Or would it be helpful to hire someone with specific competencies that would benefit your company? Consider education, special skills, advanced knowledge? What other resources within the community can you identify that will strengthen your market position? What could you import into your community or business that would make you stronger? Do you have significant support in the community, Better Business Bureau, Rotary Club, Chamber of Commerce, Outreach Programs? Can you create a training program for skills that would benefit you? How about a scholarship program to encourage those skills? Can you encourage your local college to add a specific subject to its elective subject curriculum?

Consider all available skills and knowledge that you and your employees have developed in previous positions or the experience of organizing and managing a company. The combination of skills, education, along with a knowledge and interest in the field, certainly provides you with strengths that can help you succeed.

Identify the practical skills and abilities that you or others in your organization may possess. (See Figure 1) Keep in mind, this is not rocket science. Just get a general idea of these skills but also be as specific as you can be. You don't have to take two months to do this. You just want to identify the strengths of your organization. It should only take a few minutes. You can add other things that you come up with at a later time.

Outside Strengths

Outside strengths refer to companies with which you do business that provide products or services that you use or sell. You should evaluate these to determine if there is anything that they can do to help you do business more effectively. Even if they have to change a product or service for you, is it something that will give you an edge against your competition?

Especially consider other companies that are competing with your suppliers or service providers. Learn about what they do and how their products and services compare to what your existing suppliers are providing. Ask yourself, what can they do to help you? Can they "private label" a specific product for you that gives you an edge over the competition? Can they engage in research and development work to find a better material or product feature that they can put into your products to make them better? Can they help you improve your efficiency by training you and your employees to be more productive? What are they automating and how are their research and development efforts paying off for them? How can you avail yourself of their knowledge, and, even more importantly, can you independently upgrade their product if you can find an innovation they haven't thought about?

Strengths Analysis Checklist – Figure 1

Assess each skill by writing the term "Strong", "Average" or "Weak" in the Assessment column.

Skill	Assessment
Financial Planning	
Budgeting, Accounting, Management	
Human Resource Management	
Recruiting, Training, Supervising, Motivating Staff and Volunteers	
Safety, Security, Risk Management	
Admissions, Venue Grounds, Spectators, Players, Personnel	
Hospitality	

Invitation Design and Production, Amenities, Coordination of Logistics, Hosting Activities	
Food and Beverage	
Negotiations, Quality, Quantity, Contract and Price	
Sales and Marketing	
Prospecting, Selling, Closing, Servicing	
Writing	
Correspondence, Promotional Copy, Internal Memoranda, Newsletters, Trade Publication Articles, Media Releases, Follow-ups	
Leadership Ability	
List Additional Areas Below:	

Analysis of Strengths

The first thing to do is organize your strengths in the following order: Strong Assessments, Average Assessments and Weak Assessments. Start with the weak assessments and ask your group what ideas they have for improving each of these. Take a "Problem Solving Worksheet" and assign three or more individuals to work on these and report back at next week's meeting. Assign average assessments to another group of employees and ask them to report back next week and do likewise with Strong Assessments.

The Problem-Solving Worksheet will give your employees a tool for developing an inductive approach to the problem which will lead to a definitive solution that will be worth discussing. Make sure they are able to develop the necessary audio-visual materials, presentations, charts, business process charts, etc. that they would like to present at the next meeting.

Needless to say, your knowledge and leadership will be vital to developing workable solutions that will have a positive influence on the company. Make sure your door is open at all times for any of these team members to walk in and ask questions or hold a discussion with you. Make sure you guide this process and use it as a developmental tool for each individual. Challenge them, never settle for average and push them to go beyond the average and to excel – to find real solutions and develop the arguments necessary to defend their ideas.

At the next SWOT Meeting, give every group an equal amount of time to make his presentation. Don't assign a leader, let the leader emerge and if he takes the baton, let him know it is his baton to carry. Ask the following questions.

On weak assessments:

- Which is the one weakness whose solution will improve the company the most?
- What is the cause of that weakness?
- What can be done to solve it, to turn the weakness into a strength?
- What is the Business Process solution to this weakness? How were things done in the past and how will they be done in the future?
- Why is the proposed solution the best solution?
- What benchmarks will we use to determine success and what kind of reporting mechanism will we use and who will be responsible for the reporting?

Project Worksheet for Strengths

WEEK / DATE	DUTY AND DUE DATE	ASSIGNED TO	DATE FINISHED

SMART Goals for Strengths

Category	Definition	Result and Date of Result
Specific Goal		
Measurable Desired Result		
Achievable (Yes/No)		
Results-Focused (Yes/No)		
Time Bound		

Weaknesses

Analyzing weaknesses, though not an entertaining activity, is vital to your success because these harmful internal weaknesses can negatively impact your success as a company. First, you should convene a meeting with key staff and volunteers to determine any weaknesses that are important enough to address. Ask them to suggest internal areas that are inadequate, that may be controlled and/or corrected, or that should be eliminated before they erode your profitability.

Elimination of weaknesses may mean personnel changes, retraining or reassignment, possibly even termination of some people and hiring someone with special skills. Weaknesses and dealing with them are as important to your organization as strengths because they are the negatives that are drawing you down.

One weakness to seriously look at: Is your marketing program good enough to bring in new customers or sales?

Use Figure 2 for identifying weaknesses of your team.

The Weakness Analysis Checklist - Figure 2

Weakness	Assessment
Disagreements among key staff and/or volunteers	
Personality conflicts among staff and/or volunteers	
Lack of trained, experienced personnel and/or volunteers	
Short planning time	
Funding problems	
Facility shortage or inadequacies	

This approach of assessing your team strengths and weaknesses will help you improve your organization and enable you to handle the opportunities and threats from both inside and outside sources. This is critical to the survival of your company and your future success. If you don't know what is wrong, you don't know how to fix it. If you don't know your weaknesses, you don't know how to turn them into strengths. This is what I call focused management and it is much better than just plodding along, don't you think?

On weak assessments:

Which is the one weakness whose solution will improve the company the most?

What is the cause of that weakness?

What can be done to solve it, to turn the weakness into a strength?

What is the Business Process solution to this weakness? How were things done in the past and how will they be done in the future?

Why is the proposed solution the best solution?

What benchmarks will we use to determine success and what kind of reporting mechanism will you use and who will be responsible for the reporting?

Project Worksheet for Weaknesses

WEEK/ DATE	DUTY AND DUE DATE	ASSIGNED TO	DATE FINISHED

SMART Goals for Weaknesses

Category	Definition	Result and Date of Result
Specific Goal		
Measurable Desired Result		
Achievable (Yes/No)		

Results-Focused (Yes/No)		
Time Bound		

Opportunities

The opportunities that present themselves may increase your revenues, but what are these opportunities? How can you recognize them, anticipate them and plan for them?

- Local Opportunities – Your local area has a strong base of businesses with which you can develop strong relationships – find out how to meet the necessary people and where to hang out so you can meet the Who's Who in local influence. These are all good people to know. As I mentioned above, a good place to start is your local golf club. One executive I knew years ago told me he got lots of his clients by sitting at the bar of his golf club one or two nights a week. You might be surprised who shows up at places where people gather for fun and relaxation.

- Don't forget social networking sites. I've had lots of my Facebook friends turn into clients because I sometimes posted work my company had done for other clients. You can create your own social media network and meet lots of new people by careful postings on Facebook, Twitter and/or LinkedIn.com. Don't forget local business groups such as Kiwanis, Toastmasters and others where you can meet intelligent and industrious people intent on self-improvement and making good connections. Your local Chamber of Commerce and other similar organizations can be helpful as well.

- Events as opportunities – Every event you participate in or put on, and even those you don't, often present opportunities to meet people who can help you, or people with whom you can network. Are you ready for these opportunities? Do you have a plan to pursue them and take advantage of them?

You will want to qualify all opportunities as "HOT" (action required), "GREEN" (investigate further) and "LUKEWARM" (possible but not immediate need). Finally, determine whether an opportunity requires action on your part to make it happen.

Use Figure 3 to identify the opportunities for your business.

Opportunity	Assessment
Each planned event (list below – include Trade Shows, Seminars, Job Fairs, etc.)	
New Opportunities (list below)	

Opportunities you have identified should each support your goals and objectives. If one does not *entirely* support your end result, determine ways to control it or get rid of it. For example, a tourist-related activity such as a major music festival may be scheduled on the same date as your concert or sporting event. Control this activity to the best of your ability by giving your local fans and sponsors something special that day so they come to your event rather than the festival. Or have flyers passed out at the festival telling people about your event to see how many decide to do both. If they present the flyer at a place of your designation, give them a freebie for coming. Otherwise, this scheduling conflict could become a threat rather than an opportunity.

Additional suggestions:

There may be opportunities of which you are unaware and the world of the Internet can provide you with valuable information about new opportunities. I would suggest that you use the following keywords on your favorite search engine:

Trade Shows

Seminars

Sales Training

Press Releases (in your industry)

Open Projects and Grant Opportunities

Also use keywords that are typical in your industry.

I would even recommend having one of your marketing employees check these and other keywords every day and report his or her findings to the VP of Marketing. You might be surprised about what you can discover that will be very valuable to your revenues.

Project Worksheet for Opportunities

WEEK/ DATE	DUTY AND DUE DATE	ASSIGNED TO	DATE FINISHED

SMART Goals for Opportunities

Category	Definition	Result and Date of Result
Specific Goal		
Measurable Desired Result		
Achievable (Yes/No)		
Results-Focused (Yes/No)		

Time Bound		

Threats

Threats of all types may jeopardize the success of your business. By recognizing potential threats, you gain the advantage of planning ahead and blocking these threats from harming your business.

To determine the range of threats to your success, bring together all team members for a threat analysis meeting. This includes risk management, volunteers, marketing people, mechanics, engineers, technicians and all other critical people.

Ask each employee to list any potential threats within their area of responsibility and identify any threats that may affect the team as a whole. I've always told my people, if you give me a problem, bring the solution with you. That will help motivate them to make a contribution. See Figure 4.

The Threats Analysis Checklist Figure 4

Threats	Comments and Solutions (Criteria: Serious, Monitor Further, Requires Action
Personnel	
Business Processes	
Rules and Regulations	
Financial Concerns	
Sales	
Management	
Customer Service	
Other Threats (list)	

Now that you've finished your SWOT Analysis, enlist your team in a project that will assign an action, a completion date and a "report-back" date for each initiative you will assign to them. Keep records of all this and set schedule items for yourself to follow up on all acts and ascertain how things are going.

Project Worksheet for Threats

WEEK / DATE	DUTY AND DUE DATE	ASSIGNED TO	DATE FINISHED

SMART Goals for Threats

Category	Definition	Result and Date of Result
Specific Goal		

Measurable Desired Result		
Achievable (Yes/No)		
Results-Focused (Yes/No)		
Time Bound		

Decision-Making Worksheet

Every decision you make should be based upon the relevant facts of the situation that give rise to the need for a decision. These facts can be broken down into positive statements (propositions and conclusions) that can be checked against reality (proven). You arrive at these conclusions and propositions by means of investigation (also called induction).

Effective decision-making can only take place when you use the best available knowledge. The jump from your knowledge to the correct decision is much easier if you apply the principles we discussed in our chapters on logic and logical fallacies.

Decision-making can only be based upon induction and analysis of the facts of reality as they relate to the field upon which you must decide. Essentially, there are three steps:

1. Identify the question about which the decision is to be made, and
2. Identify the facts that relate to that question, and
3. Draw your conclusion.

Decision-Making Worksheet

Decision-Making Worksheet
Date:
Individuals involved in this decision
Question
Relevant Facts
Needed Knowledge
How Will You Apply this Knowledge?

What tests or analyses will I need to make?
Results of test or analysis – list as bullet points
Decision (give reasons)

Who will implement the decision?
How will the decision be implemented?
When will the decision be implemented?
Who will be responsible for maintaining any necessary actions and to whom will they report?

Problem Solving Worksheet

In this section, we refer to business problems that haunt the company. They can be such things as inefficient business processes, the use of faulty equipment in production, personnel policies and standards of quality, etc. Such problems cause a business to lose money, perform disappointingly or harm company morale. When a business problem is solved, the company becomes stronger and improves its standing with customers.

As an employee, you add value to the company when you consider yourself part of the solution rather than part of the problem. Problem solving is a skill that all the best managers have. They don't hold back and they never settle for situations that keep the company from fulfilling its mission.

The first thing to do to solve a business problem is to describe the problem and the negative consequences of the problem. Quantify these consequences if possible. Then, use the process of induction to identify a solution that has a "possible" better consequence.

Implementing the solution is also very important. Someone should be charged with the responsibility for taking the actions that will solve the problem and a reporting process should be maintained. As this process moves forward, adjustments should be made as needed to improve the solution and focus it specifically on the problem.

It is always important to realize that it is the boss's or owner's responsibility to sanction your work and make the final decision to change procedures and fix the problem. Make sure you have his or her blessing for anything you do to solve the problem.

Problem Solving Worksheet

Problem Solving Worksheet
Date:
Individuals involved in this investigation
Problem
Statistics or Measurement Criteria
What is the Specific Cause of this Problem?

What is the Specific Business Process that is affected by this Problem?

Describe the Steps of this Business Process

What Specific Step is Responsible for this Problem?

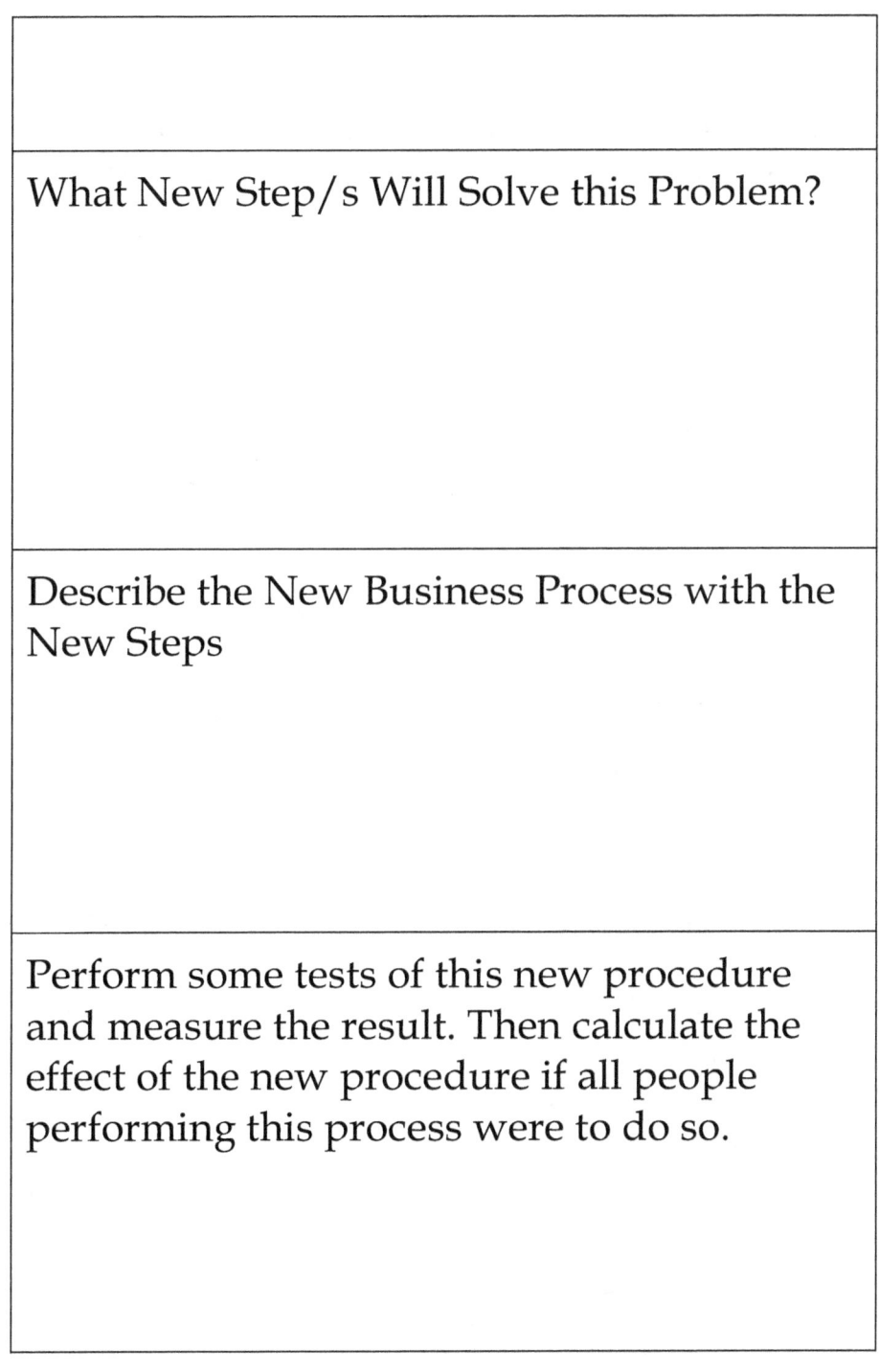

Meet with and Report Results to the Director in Charge. Report the Results of the Meeting Here:
Next Step: (Do Another Worksheet or Implement the Procedure Company-Wide)

SWOT Analysis as a Performance Review

You can use a SWOT Analysis to investigate company-wide problems or specific problems that plague a department or small group of employees. You can also use a SWOT Analysis as a Performance Review for an individual. Such a review would have the added benefit of not only evaluating the employee but also giving him or her a plan for improving their performance based upon the employee's chosen areas for improvement and helping to set a follow up for him or her within a few months. Below are the four steps that I recommend for a Performance Review. Of course, you can also create one specific to the tasks that any individual must address in his or her own performance.

Strengths

Weaknesses

Opportunities

Threats

Once you have identified each element then the next step is to identify what the employee must do in order to deal with each element.

Element	Characteristics	Planned Action and Date	Date Completed
Strengths			
Weaknesses			
Opportunities			
Threats			

The Personal SWOT Analysis

The SWOT Analysis can also provide the foundation for your personal and career development. A well-thought-out SWOT Analysis can keep you on track in your career and keep you ahead of the game when it comes to the expectations of your boss. I'd also recommend your obtaining a copy of my book: "How to be a Great Employee and a Better Manager".

Personal SWOT Analysis

Element	Characteristics	Planned Action and Date	Date Completed
Strengths			

Weaknesses			
Opportunities			
Threats			

Conclusion

Companies that don't change don't survive. Change can come after recognizing a competitor's success or by careful planning through tools such as the SWOT Analysis, SMART goals and well-documented project management. It pays to become proficient at changing to meet your customers' needs. If you have any questions about this booklet, don't hesitate to send an email to **robertsswot@outlook.com**. If we add your ideas to this book, we will give you credit and link to your website. If you have a great success story, perhaps we can profile your experience in future versions of this publication or on our website.

Much success to you.

Business Books by Robert Villegas

These four books by Robert Villegas comprise some of the business books that he has written. As an executive working for several companies, he was able to develop these methods that will help anyone seeking to excel in the business world. These books are:

How to Be a Great Employee – and a Greater Manager

You cannot be a great manager without first being a great employee. And this is something that requires learning, experience and attitude. The attitude comes from you but the learning and experience you should acquire through diligent study and practice. http://amzn.to/2BqdG2i $3.99 Kindle $8.95 softcover

SWOT Analysis Supercharged

A SWOT Analysis is an objective look at the internal and external elements of your organization that impact your success or lack thereof. If done diligently, you will always have a handle on what you need to do to improve season after season. http://amzn.to/2BCAWYx $3.99 Kindle $6.95 softcover

The Five-Module Call Center Training System

The Five-Module Call Center Training System is designed to assist the Call Center Team Leader in helping his employees quickly upgrade their skills to an acceptable level. http://amzn.to/2B3Svj1 $3.99 Kindle $5.95 softcover

Website Development Methodology

Effective strategic marketing requires the ability to differentiate the website development organization and its deliverables from those of the competition. http://amzn.to/2DnYMqh $2.99 Kindle $12.95 softcover.

www.robertvillegas.com

Alcoholism and Addiction – the System

These four books comprise a system that can be used by both patients and counselors who are battling Alcoholism and Addiction. Based upon Mr. Villegas's own system developed during his struggle against alcoholism, this system includes:

Alcoholism and Addiction – A Secular Ten-Step Program
This groundbreaking book offers a secular approach to alcoholism unlike that offered by Alcoholics Anonymous. We recommend that every individual going for alcohol and drug-abuse counseling be given a copy of this book which contains the workbook and the two versions of The World's first drunk. http://amzn.to/2md6R9w $3.45 Kindle $11.95 softcover

The Secular Ten-Step Program Workbook
This booklet covers the program developed by Mr. Villegas. It is designed as a workbook with blank spaces for the patient to write his own thoughts as he takes each of the ten steps. Order one copy for each patient in counseling. http://amzn.to/2lrHimS $4.49 Kindle $6.95 softcover

The World's First Drunk – With Counselor Talking Points
This booklet is designed for the counselor as he works with patients during individual or group therapy. It contains helpful tips on discussing the life story of the man who invented alcohol. Order one copy for each patient in counseling. http://amzn.to/2l446Wr $2.99 Kindle $5.95 softcover

The World's First Drunk – Patient Version
This version of the short story contains empty spaces where the patient can answer questions about the life story of the man who invented alcohol. Order one copy for each counselor. http://amzn.to/2ldxBGb $2.99 Kindle $5.95 softcover.

www.robertvillegas.com

The REAL Purpose-Driven Life

The REAL Purpose-Driven Life
After centuries of being told that it is not about you, it is time to set the record straight. You are a unique individual and your goal in life should be to achieve your own happiness.
https://amzn.to/2XyrpPf $3.50 Kindle $7.95 softcover

Values and Purpose Workbook
This book is about you. It's about time. After centuries of being told that nothing is about you, it is time to set the record straight. You are a unique individual and your goal in life should be to achieve your happiness. https://amzn.to/2XwlkTv $3.99 Kindle $8.95 softcover

www.robertvillegas.com

Values and Purpose Books by Robert Villegas

The Real Purpose-Driven Life
After centuries of being told that it is not about you, it is time to set the record straight. You are a unique individual and your goal in life should be to achieve your own happiness. This book is about helping you accomplish your goals and fixing your purpose firmly in place. It covers not only why you should pursue your goals but how to do it. https://amzn.to/3ebkhjr $3.99 Kindle $6.95 softcover

The Values and Purpose Workbook
Rather than give you tasks that involve doing a lot of things for other people, I'm am going to tell you that focusing on yourself will reveal your life's purpose and express your passions and freedom. I'm going to start with you. https://amzn.to/3eQf4wG $2.99 Kindle $6.95 softcover

This Book is About You
Some people move briskly bent on a purpose, concerned only about what they are about. People walk by them; they don't even notice. They just keep to their path and you wonder where they are going. This book is about you. It's about time. https://amzn.to/3vFMzss $6299 Kindle $5.95 softcover

www.robertvillegas.com

Self-Help Books by Robert Villegas

Existence a Rational Thoughtbook
A Rational Thoughtbook is designed for thinking as opposed to reading. It combines brief prescient content with stunning imagery. Existence focuses on the nature of existence and gives you intelligent thoughts to integrate into your life.
https://amzn.to/2RZpsKV $4.99 Kindle $12.95 softcover

The Virtue of Independence
One of the most important goals for any person is to establish intellectual independence. Intellectual independence is the road to "life" independence, which is the ability to earn your own way without help from others. https://amzn.to/3awuCV2 $2.99 Kindle $6.95 softcover

Rational Meditation
Rational Meditation is self-meditation. It is thinking about yourself without guilt and without the tenets of modern philosophy (that the world is unknowable, that man is a phony, that ethics and living are only about others). https://amzn.to/3gus9OE $6.99 Kindle $12.95 softcover

History of My Mind
This booklet is the companion to my book entitled Rational Meditation. It utilizes the various exercises of the original book that involve contemplation or meditation and provide space for written input by the reader. https://amzn.to/3gy3hpl $4.69 Kindle $11.95 softcover.

www.robertvillegas.com

Rational Thoughtbooks by Robert Villegas

Existence a Rational Thoughtbook
A Rational Thoughtbook is designed for thinking as opposed to reading. It combines brief prescient content with stunning imagery. Existence focuses on the nature of existence and gives you intelligent thoughts to integrate into your life.
https://amzn.to/2RZpsKV $4.99 Kindle $12.95 softcover

Identity
One of the most important goals for any person is to establish intellectual independence. Intellectual independence is the road to "life" independence, which is the ability to earn your own way without help from others. https://amzn.to/3nf9aJn $3.99 Kindle $9.95 softcover

www.robertvillegas.com

Books on Psychology and Virtue

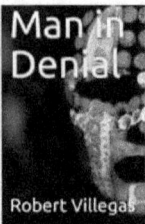   

Man in Denial
If psychology has no solid epistemology and metaphysics, how can it stand on its own? I do not think it can and this explains why psychology is in such a sad state today. Yet, before we can put psychology on a solid foundation, philosophy too must advance above the level of puberty. With its base in modern philosophy, even philosophy cannot stand on its own which exposes the real problems with modern psychology. https://amzn.to/3oVTDAQ $5.99 Kindle $9.95 softcover $18.95 hardcover

Understanding the Modern Mind
The purpose of this book is to delve into critical issues about how the human mind has come to the modern position of doubt and despair. The culprits in this matter include the irrationality of both rationalism and skepticism, and, in particular, the child of skepticism known as pragmatism.
https://amzn.to/3mRLZF9 $6.99 Kindle $9.60 softcover $26.95 hardcover

How Marcuse Destroyed Capitalism
One of the fathers of critical theory was Herbert Marcuse who escaped European dictatorship only by coming to America. America gave him the freedom and protection he needed to destroy capitalism in America.
https://amzn.to/2YW9LaS $4.99 Kinde $8.95 softcover.

The Logical Fallacy of Altruism
A logical fallacy is a faulty thought process that violates a rule of proper thinking. Correct arguments are defined as proper generalized expressions that define logical truths or knowledge. In effect, a rule of logical reasoning addresses all of the common modes of valid argument while the faulty argument contradicts them. This book examines altruism as a logical fallacy.
https://amzn.to/3vdFiB0 $5.99 Kindle $9.95 softcover $18.95 Hardcover

www.robertvillegas.com

Books on Sport and Entertainment Sponsorship

Finding Sponsors 1 and 2
This book is written for anyone seeking sponsorship relationships in the sport and entertainment fields. The ideas and principles presented here are applicable to any company, sport team, entertainment company, marketing agency and charitable organization that uses corporate sponsorships to support its activities. Volume 1: https://amzn.to/3ejm1Hp $5.19 Kindle $12.95 softcover Volume 2: https://amzn.to/3eVDo0e $4.69 Kindle $10.95 softcover

How to Write a Sponsorship Proposal
This booklet provide you with some basic guidelines on what to communicate in order to produce a winning sponsorship proposal. These guidelines will focus on what you should be presenting to your potential sponsor to make the best business case for involvement with your team or entertainment company. $2.99 Kindle $6.95 softcover

Hospitality Event Planning Handbook
One key part of your sponsorship activation strategy might be customer hospitality events in conjunction with sporting events. How do you pull off a Hospitality Event for your biggest customers? You may not know how to start, what to do and how to ensure the event is a success. This book can help. http://amzn.to/2mxzpgy $7.95 softcover.

Selling Sponsorship in the Age of the Coronavirus
This book provides suggestions on how sport teams, athletes and concert promoters can mitigate the damage done to their businesses by the economic lockdowns (due to the Coronavirus). It integrates checklists, SWOT Analysis and other valuable business aids into one toolkit that will help you keep your sport and/or genre alive in these difficult times. https://amzn.to/2QVBNiM $5.15 Kindle $5.95 softcover

www.robertvillegas.com

Books on Sponsorship and Business

Finding Sponsors Forms Book
This "Forms Book" is intended to provide samples of the forms mentioned in my book "Finding Sponsors for Sport and Entertainment". This will make it possible for you to reproduce these forms in other formats as well as download the forms document from the SponsorProAZ website for use with Microsoft Word.
https://amzn.to/3b95yDW $2.99 Kindle $5.50 softcover

Submitting Your Sponsorship Proposal Online
This booklet enables sport teams and concert promoters to submit their sponsorship proposals to companies that accept only online submission of proposals. https://amzn.to/3euzdti $2.99 Kindle $5.95 softcover

The Art of Sponsorship
This short book is based upon Mr. Villegas' book "Finding Sponsors for Sport and Entertainment". It is also based upon a course that he taught for an organization managing Indiana Parks and Recreation facilities. It is, in a sense, a condensation of information from the book geared toward organizations that would like to earn revenues on their facilities through corporate sponsorship.
https://amzn.to/3beuVnC $2.99 Kinde $6.95 softcover.

Restarting Your Business After the Pandemic
This new book is designed to help you restart your business after the Coronavirus pandemic. You will find here all the right questions, how you can find the answers and the forms you need to walk through your restart and coming success. https://amzn.to/2QVBNiM $5.15 Kindle $5.95 softcover

www.robertvillegas.com

www.ingramcontent.com/pod-product-compliance
Lightning Source LLC
Chambersburg PA
CBHW050019230526
45470CB00003B/1033